THE KID'S GUIDE TO CAMPING

Eileen Ogintz

FALCONGUIDES®

Guilford, Connecticut

Thanks to Kampgrounds of America (KOA) for facilitating this project and enabling families to enjoy the outdoors, however they choose to camp. Thanks also to the National Park Service, my camping-loving daughters Regina Foldes and Melanie Yemma for their suggestions, and all of the kids around the country who offered their input.

All the information in this guidebook is subject to change. We recommend that you call ahead to obtain current information before traveling.

FALCONGUIDES®

An imprint of The Rowman & Littlefield Publishing Group, Inc.
4501 Forbes Blvd., Ste. 200
Lanham, MD 20706
www.rowman.com
Falcon and FalconGuides are registered trademarks and Make Adventure Your Story is a trademark of The Rowman & Littlefield Publishing Group, Inc.

Distributed by NATIONAL BOOK NETWORK

Select camping content provided by Kampgrounds of America, Inc.

British Library Cataloguing in Publication Information available

Library of Congress Cataloging-in-Publication Data

Names: Ogintz, Eileen, author.
Title: The kid's guide to camping / Eileen Ogintz.
Description: Guilford, Connecticut : Falcon, 2021. | Summary: "A kid's guide to camping. Includes break-out boxes; tips for parents and for/from kids; interactive games, puzzles, and coloring pages; and more"— Provided by publisher.
Identifiers: LCCN 2020043405 (print) | LCCN 2020043406 (ebook)
ISBN 9781493057887 (paperback) | ISBN 9781493057894 (epub)
Subjects: LCSH: Camping—Juvenile literature. | Outdoor life—Juvenile literature.
Classification: LCC GV191.7 .O45 2021 (print) | LCC GV191.7 (ebook) | DDC 796.54—dc23
LC record available at https://lccn.loc.gov/2020043405
LC ebook record available at https://lccn.loc.gov/2020043406
The paper used in this publication meets the minimum requirements of American National Standard for Information Sciences—Permanence of Paper for Printed Library Materials, ANSI/NISO Z39.48-1992.

Contents

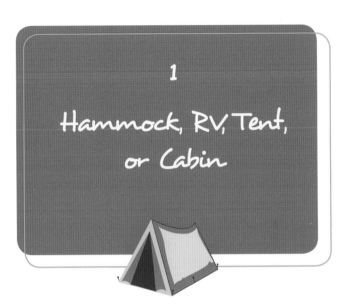

1

Hammock, RV, Tent, or Cabin

Ready?

Ready to head outdoors to skip rocks in the river, hike in the woods, bike down a mountain trail, or sleep under the stars?

Who cares if you get dirty? Who cares if you wear the same T-shirt for three days? No wonder most kids love to go camping!

Find a campground anywhere in the country through a company like Kampgrounds of America (KOA, pronounced K-O-A) and choose from a range of sites to match your family's style.

You can carry all your gear in a backpack and head into the wilderness.

If that sounds too hard, you can camp right near your car snuggling in a sleeping bag.

Sleep in a hammock strung between trees, in a tent, or outdoors under the stars. Swim in a lake, a river, or a campground pool. Soak in a natural hot spring or a campground hot tub.

A lot of families like to travel in an RV or use a camper they pull behind the car. Your parents can rent one to see if that would suit your camping style. You have a place to play when it rains, a comfy

DID YOU KNOW?

There are lots of ways to camp besides in a tent. You can camp in an RV, a cabin, or under the stars, like many do in warm places such as the Grand Canyon. Some campgrounds, are more like resorts with swimming pools, hot tubs, shops, and organized kids' activities.

bed, bathroom, and plenty of room for all the toys and games you want to bring. Your mom and dad can make meals whenever you're hungry because there's a mini fridge and cooktop. And since the RV goes wherever you do, you're never without your stuff, whether you need a rain jacket, a fleece, or a snack.

If your family members are camping newbies, you might want to go to a campground that has cabins. Some are pretty fancy!

Of course, the best part of camping is getting outdoors—hiking and fishing and biking, exploring national parks and famous and not-so-famous places. Here is your chance to climb to the top of a waterfall or explore a cave! Maybe you'll catch dinner in a nearby river!

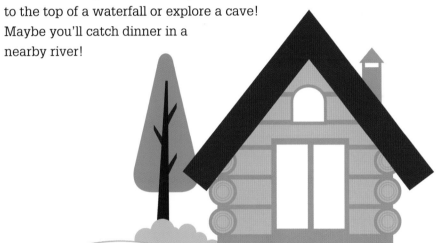

A KOA MONTANA CAMPING KID SAYS:
"My favorite is to camp in a cabin because you still get to be outdoors while having a roof over your head."
—KK, 12

You'll be having so much fun that you won't miss TV, video games, or texting with your friends—not much anyway!

And when you're done with your adventure of the day, you'll still have lots of fun—playing cards, helping to cook over an open fire, racing around on your scooter or your bike, kicking around a soccer ball, playing catch, and telling scary stories around the campfire.

You'll meet lots of other kids too, even from other countries. Maybe you can practice whatever language you are learning in school.

A COLORADO KID SAYS:
"You always get to meet kids at a campground."
—Stella, 10

Does your family have a dog? Most families bring their pooches when they camp. Dogs love being outside as much as you do! Many bring cats too.

{ What's Cool? Doing something on a camping trip you've never done. Have you ever hiked to the top of a waterfall? Gone mountain biking?

What Do You See?

The night sky can be especially bright when you are camping. Check out the **International Dark Sky Places Program** (darksky.org) that designates lands that have really terrific starry nights. They include **Arches National Park** (nps.gov/arch) in Utah, **Big Bend National Park** (nps.gov/bibe) in Texas, and **Joshua Tree National Park** (nps.gov/jotr) in California.

You may see so many stars you'll have trouble identifying the ones you know! Can you see:

- The Milky Way?
- A planet?
- A cluster of stars?
- A constellation?

Download an app to help, like the **NASA app** (nasa.gov/nasaapp) or one from **SkySafari** or **SkyView Lite** in the App Store. Binoculars always help too!

DID YOU KNOW?

There are more than a million new campers every year. Are you one of them?

Learn the Lingo

You may be wondering if the campers you meet are speaking a different language, especially if you are new to camping. Here's a KOA lingo list:

- **Bear canister:** The National Park Service allows campers to use hard-sided containers only, such as bear canisters, for food storage.

- **Billy:** A billy, or billy can, is small metal container used to boil water or cook food over a campfire. Billy cans typically have a handle on the top for convenient campfire cooking, but makeshift billy cans may also be made out of coffee cans or other metal containers. The billy originated in Australia and has since become a recognized symbol for bush culture.

- **Boondocking:** Also called "dry camping," boondocking is RV camping in remote campsites without electricity, water, or sewer hookups.

- **Carabiner:** A metal clip with a spring gate that campers use to clip a water bottle to a backpack. They come in all sorts of colors!

- **Dome:** Dome is one of the most common tent shapes with light-weight aluminum tent poles.

- **Full hookup:** RV campsites that are described as "full hookup" sites will have access to the campground's electric, water, and sewer supplies. KOA is known for these sites.

- **Hula skirt:** When traveling on rocky or dusty roads, RVs can kick up a lot of debris and stones. A hula skirt can be attached to the rear bumper of an RV to prevent this debris from hitting vehicles behind the trailer.

- **Guylines:** Guylines are cables used to add stability to tents; they can be attached to the rain fly and then staked to the ground or tied to nearby trees.

- **Potable:** Potable water is drinking water that is safe to consume without any other treatment.

DID YOU KNOW?

A cairn is a small stack of rocks that may be used to mark a trail. Cairns are often used in areas where there are no trees. The term *cairn* comes from the Gaelic for "heap of stones." Cairns have been used around the world to guide explorers and mark trails throughout history. But don't build your own, as it can disturb the surrounding area.

- **Rig:** This is what campers call RVs.

- **Slide-out:** Some RVs have slide-outs that can be pushed out to expand the available living space and then retracted when traveling.

- **Snowbird:** *Snowbird* is a term used to describe RVers who head south in the winter to escape colder weather up north. Many KOA campgrounds are open year-round across the country, so campers can migrate to any climate they want to enjoy the winter.

- **Toy hauler:** A toy hauler is an RV that can carry motorcycles, ATVs, and other big outdoor "toys."

- **Underbelly:** The floor surface or underside of an RV is often called the underbelly. The RV underbelly includes water hoses, pipes, and other valves. In the winter, RVers who hope to keep using their RV often add protective material to the underbelly.

Tell the Adults: KOA Locations

Families these days say they camp for the chance to get the kids outdoors, rather than because it is the most inexpensive lodging option. During the pandemic, many families have opted for RVs and cabins so they have private bathrooms and cooking facilities.

Many campgrounds these days, in fact, are more like hotels and vacation resorts with pools, mini golf, organized activities, on-site grocery stores, coffee bars, restaurants, and shuttles into town. You can rent a cabin or park your RV if you don't want to tent camp. Many also offer services to connect you with locals, whether you want to go mountain biking or river rafting, or take an off-road jeep tour.

There are more than 500 **KOA** locations across North America— you can find one in nearly any state and Canada! KOA is the world's largest system of open-to-the-public campgrounds, with camping options any family can make their own.

KOA Journey campgrounds, located near major highways and byways of North America, are designed for convenience with long pull-thru RV sites. These campgrounds make it easy for stopovers to your final destination with well-lit night registration and robust RV supplies.

DID YOU KNOW?

The first KOA campground was founded on the banks of the Yellowstone River in Billings, Montana, in 1964. The campground and the corporate office are still located there today.

KOA Holidays are an ideal place to relax and play with plenty to do and amenities and services like pools and jumping pillows. Enjoy the outdoor experience even more with upgraded RV sites with a **KOA Patio**® and deluxe cabins with full baths for camping in comfort. A 250-square-foot-plus KOA Patio site comes equipped with outdoor furniture, a fire pit or fire ring, and a grill. There's no better place to wake up and enjoy a cup of coffee with the sunrise.

And for your pooch, **KampK9**® **dog parks** provide a fenced area with cleanup stations, fresh water, and, in some cases, dedicated areas for large and small dogs. These are great places where your pup can play off-leash.

KOA Resorts are your recreation destinations. With resort-style pools, activity directors, and food service, you'll never have to leave the campground. These campgrounds also have RV sites and deluxe cabins with a KOA Patio®. From diamond mines to palm trees, each KOA Resort has the quality amenities and services adults rely on with their own theme that brings them to life.

Staying Safe in a Campground

Kids like camping because their parents will give them more freedom to explore a campground than they might at a hotel. But you still need to follow certain rules to stay safe:

- Ask permission before wandering away from your campsite.

- Practice "what if" you get lost with your parents or can't reach them.

- You probably have your parents' cell phone numbers in your phone, if you have one. But you may not always have good cell service when you are camping. Keep their numbers on a card with you, just in case.

- If you can't reach them, look for someone in a uniform to help you.

CAMPGROUND TIP
At KOA Campgrounds, you always know the staff because they wear yellow!

{ **What's Cool?** Playing music around the campfire. Don't forget a harmonica!

A MAINE KID SAYS:

"We go camping at state parks and other places. I like it best if there is a pool or especially a lake so we can go swimming and fishing and kayaking."
—Mike, 14

WELCOME TO THE CAMPSITE!

Fill in the missing letters to spell out the mystery words. (You will need to use some of the secret letters twice!)

(___)OY HAULER
(3)

GUY L(___)NES
(2)

FULL (___)OOKUP
(5)

(___)OTABLE
(1)

B(___)AR BAG
(7)

(___)ARABINER
(4)

KO(___) CAMPGROUND
(6)

S(___)OWBIRD
(8)

___ ___ ___ ___ ___   ___   ___ ___ ___ ___
(1) (2) (3) (4) (5)   (6)   (3) (7) (8) (3)

See page 118 for the answers!

CONNECT THE DOTS!

Follow the dots with your pencil to reveal one vital part of your outdoor adventure!

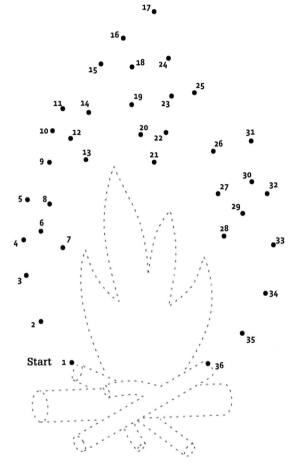

What is it? __ __ __ __ __ __ __ __

See page 118 for the answer!

2

Road Trip!

Have your pillow?

A comfy blanket would be nice. So would some snacks and stuff to do.

You'll have plenty of room to play in an RV. But it's not so bad if you need to share a back seat in the car with your brother or sister. You can even mark your space with some masking tape—use it to draw some designs on the seat in front of you.

Now you are ready to hit the road. Whether you are traveling in an RV, a car, or a car pulling a camper, you are going to log miles on the road getting to your favorite camping spots. Luckily, you'll likely stop at some places along the way—a national park, maybe a historic site or two, a museum or a zoo, maybe a place to swim. (Keep your swimsuit and towel within easy reach!)

How can you help your parents to make the road trip part of the adventure?

A WYOMING KID SAYS:
"When we're on a road trip, I'm on my phone, sleeping, or looking out the window."
—Pearl, 12

Offer to help plan! Suggest picnic lunches rather than fast-food stops. If you're in an RV, you've got a stocked mini kitchen, of course. But if you will be traveling in a car, you'll want to help pack the cooler. You can help make the shopping list! What would you want to eat if you were planning a picnic? It can't be all desserts either!

How about a grab bag with surprises you can choose every time you enter a new state?

Sure, you have video games and movies to watch on various devices, maybe a smartphone, but it would be more fun for everyone if you can think up some things everyone can do—even the driver.

Maybe you can get your parents to understand why kids love popular books by listening to audio versions. Maybe you can find an audiobook about kids in the region where you are visiting (your local librarian can help!).

DID YOU KNOW?
Most American families hit the road rather than fly for vacation.

A MINNESOTA KID SAYS:
"I listened to all the Harry Potter books while we were driving."
—Cam, 13

{ What's Cool? Listening to an audiobook with your family on a road trip. What would you pick?

Make a playlist of your favorite songs for the road. Need some inspiration? Check out the Kampgrounds of America (KOA) Spotify playlist called "Campfire Nights" and crank up the volume and sing along.

Ask your parents to show you the route you'll be traveling, so you can find some fun stops along the way. A tip: If you search the state's tourism website, you'll get some ideas. A quick Internet search can also help if you are going through a town and want to find a dog park, a playground, or a place to stop for ice cream. It's so much easier— and quicker—to find the stops you want these days!

If your family plans to stop at a state or national park, look it up so you will know a good place for a (short) hike so everyone can stretch their legs. Maybe you can walk to a waterfall or to see some ancient petroglyphs. Got a Frisbee or soccer ball?

Suggest a stop at a local museum or zoo. A lot of times, they are a great introduction to a region you might not know much about.

Are you there yet? Admit it—you were having too much fun to realize how long you'd been traveling.

DID YOU KNOW?

RVing is popular in Britain and Europe, but they call RVs "caravans."

Free Apps for the Road

Let's have some fun along the way.

Sing along with **Spotify** (spotify.com) or **Smule** (smule.com). You can even record yourselves singing and make your own music video.

Listen to audiobooks from your local library with **Libby by OverDrive** (overdrive.com). See if you can find one set in the area where you are traveling.

Play Road Trip Bingo and Trivia Crack.

Find a campground with the KOA Camping app.

Learn some geography with **Geo Touch,** where you can find out all sorts of stuff about the states you are driving through. You can find the app in the App Store.

A KOA MICHIGAN CAMPING KID SAYS:
"I love everything about camping."
—Angelo, 9, Emmett KOA Holiday

Route 66

You may know Route 66 from the *Cars* movies, cartoons, and Cars Land at Disney California Adventure. Radiator Springs is a fictional town, based on places on Route 66 between Arizona and California.

But it is also the most famous road in America, spanning nearly 2,500 miles. **Route 66** (historic66.com) was one of the country's first highways, built almost 100 years ago. It originally started in Chicago and ran through Missouri, Kansas, Oklahoma, Texas, New Mexico, and Arizona, ending in southern California.

On a road trip, it's fun to get off the highway on a road like Route 66 and go through small towns, stop for ice cream or pie at a diner, and maybe visit a local attraction like the **giant milk bottle** atop a tiny building in Oklahoma City (2426 N. Classen Blvd., if you need directions).

How many strange sites can you count along the way?

DID YOU KNOW?

Route 66 starts right in the middle of Chicago. It ends in Santa Monica, California, covering 2,448 miles.

Five Epic Road Trips

Are you a good navigator? Even if you have GPS on the road, it can be fun to follow the route you're taking on a map. Look for fun places to stop along the way! Maybe you want to swim or explore an old battlefield, take a hike or a bike ride, or have a picnic. KOA says these five road trips are guaranteed to please:

A KOA ARKANSAS KID SAYS:
"We take our cat with us. She loves riding on the motor home dash. You should see the looks we get from other cars!"
—Brittaney, 12

- The **Blue Ridge Parkway** (blueridgeparkway.org) between Virginia and North Carolina will take you through some of the oldest mountains and rivers in the world—and an especially cool waterfall.

- The **Overseas Highway** (fla-keys.com) includes 113 miles and 42 bridges that link the US mainland through the Florida Keys. Take time to snorkel and fish along the way.

- The **Pacific Coast Highway** travels from San Francisco to San Diego. Stop at the **Monterey Bay Aquarium** (montereybay aquarium.org), **Big Sur** (bigsurcalifornia.org), and **Huntington Beach** (surfcityusa.com)!

- **Grand Circle** (grandcircle.org) is a 1,500-mile loop through the desert Southwest leading to six national parks—Zion, Bryce, Capitol Reef, Arches, Canyonlands and the North Rim of the Grand Canyon. Ready for some mountain biking?

- **Great River Road** (experiencemississippiriver.com) runs from northern Minnesota to the Gulf of Mexico on both sides of the Mississippi River for 3,000 miles through 10 states. Even a small piece of it will be fun!

Snack Attack

Whether you are in an RV or a car, you're bound to get hungry when your parents want to keep going.

No worries! Just keep a stash of snacks handy in a cooler (supplies for picnics too!) Make sure you have your own water bottle too. Sure, you want some treats (just remember chocolate might melt in the hot vehicle!), but it's good to have some healthy options too! How about:

- frozen grapes, clementines, and apple slices

- Favorite cut-up veggies like cucumbers, carrots, and celery and something to dip them in like hummus or ranch dressing (in a small plastic container)

- cheese, crackers, and pita bread

- peanut butter crackers (make your own . . . assuming no one is allergic to peanuts)

- pretzels

- your own special mixture of dried fruit, cereal, and nuts

{ **What's Cool?** Stopping for homemade ice cream on a road trip. Kids love huckleberry in Montana, butter pecan in Alabama, orange cream in Florida, peach in Georgia, and Ube (lavender-colored and made with purple yams) in Hawaii.

TELL THE ADULTS: PREVENTING MOTION SICKNESS

If your kids are prone to motion sickness on road trips:

- Talk to your doctor beforehand to see if medication is warranted. If so, make sure to give it at least an hour to start working before you get on the road.

- Avoid greasy meals the night before.

- Encourage the kids to drink plenty of water.

- Insist the kids put down their devices and look outside. Looking at the horizon can really help.

- Keep a stash of dry crackers, ginger candies, and ginger ale on hand. Ginger is a traditional remedy for nausea.

- Keep cleanup supplies handy, just in case.

A COLORADO KID SAYS:
"Camping is fun in Colorado because of all the rivers and lakes to camp by."
—Jacob, 11

WHAT DID YOU SEE ON THE ROAD?

Draw what you saw!

WHAT DO YOU SEE ON THE ROAD?

Can you spot the terms hiding here? Look for all ten!

LICENSE	PICNIC	SINGALONG
SNACKS	REST STOP	CARAVAN
AIRSTREAM	AUDIOBOOK	NAVIGATOR
NAPS		

```
H  R  E  S  T  M  V  S  A  Q
L  E  V  K  O  M  H  I  U  R
I  T  M  R  C  H  T  N  D  E
C  S  L  U  L  W  T  G  L  S
E  G  V  A  M  H  F  A  J  T
N  C  O  G  P  Y  S  L  K  S
S  V  E  W  I  G  M  O  A  T
E  K  O  M  J  U  H  N  U  O
G  P  I  C  N  I  C  G  D  P
J  M  K  Z  R  M  A  S  I  X
N  A  N  O  F  N  R  A  O  S
S  N  A  C  K  S  A  O  B  G
U  G  P  S  W  Z  V  K  O  S
C  P  S  W  U  M  A  F  O  J
S  G  S  S  E  W  N  D  K  B
N  A  V  I  G  A  T  O  R  C
E  R  S  X  T  V  F  H  Z  S
A  I  R  S  T  R  E  A  M  S
H  R  E  S  T  M  V  S  A  H
```

See page 119 for the answers!

3

Setting Up Camp— What's Your Job?

Hands up if you are ready to help!

Whether you are tent camping near your car, towing a camper, traveling by RV, backpacking, or staying in a campground cabin, there are always chores to do when you arrive at a campground or campsite.

The RV will need to be hooked up or the tent put up. In the wilderness you will need to gather wood for a fire (if fires are permitted at the campground!). If the campground has a store, you'll want to buy some firewood for the firepit.

Wet clothes need to be hung up and camp chairs set up outside. You need to set up a trash and bag and one for recycling. (Maybe you can bring along the pop-up kind and then use plastic trash bags inside (they're great for wet clothes too).

Someone will need to walk the dog—on a leash, of course!

Don't forget to slather on some sunscreen—and bug spray—before you get started.

Check with your parents about what needs to be done first. Can you scout a place for the tent?

DID YOU KNOW?

When building a campfire, many different sizes of wood must be used to get the flames going. Kindling is typically the second-smallest material used to build a fire and includes thin sticks or wood. You shouldn't use wood from elsewhere if you are making a campfire. That might spread insects and disease that could threaten an entire local forest! You can usually get firewood and kindling at the campground or at a grocery store nearby. Make sure the fire is completely out before you go to bed.

If you are experienced campers, you may already know. It helps if you take turns with chores—especially with those no one likes (washing dishes!).

Do you have a backup plan? What if it rains? What if it's too cold for the beach? You can help figure out what else you can do in advance so you will be ready with a fun idea. Maybe there is a local museum or factory to visit?

Did you know if it's really hot, you will stay a lot cooler in the tent if you take it down during the day and put it back up when the sun goes down?

Keep the duct tape handy! You can use it to fix a hole in your jacket, the tent, or your sleeping bag, and you can even use it to keep the tablecloth from blowing off the picnic table.

What's cooking? Maybe you can help with breakfast or brown-bag lunches for the hiking trail. Maybe you can make dessert for dinner.

The faster the chores get done, the more time you will have for fun.

Ready to hike to a waterfall? How about a swim in the campground pool?

Campground Pet Smarts

Many families love to camp or RV because they can bring their pets along. It's a good idea to call ahead to see if pets are permitted and if there are extra fees. Kampgrounds of America (KOA) campgrounds are pooch-friendly and all have designated dog parks. But that doesn't mean everyone at the campground loves dogs as much as you do. Here's how to make sure your dog is a good campground neighbor:

- Keep your dog leashed unless you are in a specific leash-free area.

- Never leave your dog alone, even if it is tethered.

- Do your best to keep your dog from barking—especially during the night.

- Always clean up after your dog.

- Be prepared that if your dog is a problem child—aggressive or barking all the time—you might have to find somewhere else to camp.

What's Cool? Making campground friends with kids from other cities, states, and countries.

Be a Good Neighbor

You might be camping with your family in the wilderness where no one else is nearby. But you might also be at a campground or RV park where you've got lots of camping neighbors. You'll be able to make friends with kids from around the country—and around the world! It's important to be a good neighbor.

- Always walk around campsites instead of through someone's campsite.

- Be mindful of others when you are riding your bike or scooter— just like you would be at home.

- Use "inside" voices, especially during designated quiet hours and early in the morning.

- Keep food locked up and put away. You can attract animals, and human food isn't good for them.

- Leave no trace when you leave. Visit the **Leave No Trace Website** (lnt.org) for more ideas on how to be environmentally responsible.

A KOA WASHINGTON STATE CAMPING KID SAYS: "We have a good pool. Pack your swimming suit!" —Kiera, 9, Winthrop/ N. Cascades KOA

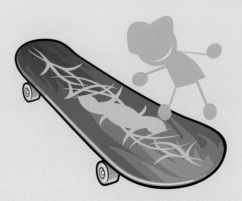

TELL THE PARENTS:
CAMPING HACKS THAT REALLY WORK

Tenting is a great way to get into camping. There are many ways to tent across the US and Canada. **KOA Tent Sites** (koa. com) offer a level, dry campsite with a solid picnic table, fire ring, and nearby restrooms and showers.

You can now find spacious **Premium Tent Sites** with large, well-defined, and comfy areas for your tent, along with ample parking and your own electric hookups for easy recharging. There's even a pole-mounted KOA "site light" that you can turn on and off. KOA also offers affordable KOA **Patio Tent Sites** to give tenters their own surfaced patio complete with gas grills, fire rings, and patio furniture.

Especially if you are a camping newbie, you'll appreciate these hacks from KOA's seasoned campers and their families:

- Rather than ice, freeze gallon jugs of water and put them in your cooler. When the ice melts, you'll have cold drinking water rather than a messy cooler.

- Corn chips and Doritos make great kindling if you can't find small sticks for your campfire. (Chip bags, however, belong in the trash.)

- Have everyone set aside a pair of socks just for sleeping. You know they will be dry and (relatively) clean!

- Use a vegetable peeler to slice individual pieces of bar soap for showers. Store them in a plastic bag so everyone can just grab one at a time.

Dry wet shoes at night by removing the insoles and stuffing them with dry, dirty clothes. The moisture will transfer from the shoes to the clothes.

If it's cold, fill empty water bottles with warm water to create makeshift hot water bottles to use near your toes. Just make sure they don't leak!

Rather than risk broken eggs, crack eggs before you leave home and store them in a water bottle. This should last several days in a mini fridge or cooler.

Five Awesome Places to Camp

Maybe you want to be in the wilderness. Maybe you'd rather be in a campground with other families and kids. You have plenty to choose from, whether you are car camping, RVing, or backpacking away from civilization. Here are five places guaranteed to please:

- **Moab, Utah,** is a great base to explore **Arches National Park** (nps.gov/arch) and **Canyonlands National Park** (nps.gov/cany) and to go hiking, rafting, and mountain biking.

- **The Pacific Coast Highway** in California runs through the redwoods and along the beaches, offering the chance to hike, explore tide pools, and hang out on beach town boardwalks. It runs along most of the Pacific coastline in California—more than 650 miles.

{ **What's Cool?** A campfire s'mores party with your campground neighbors.

- **Gaitlinburg** and **Pigeon Forge** bookend **Great Smoky Mountains National Park** (nps.gov/grsm), the most visited in the country. You can camp in the park or nearby where there's also **Dollywood** (dollywood.com), **Wonder Works** (wonderworksonline.com), dinner shows, and all the souvenir shopping you could want.

- **Page, Arizona,** is home to **Lake Powell** (lakepowell.com) with plenty of water sports, **Glen Canyon Dam** (nps.gov/glca), and amazing rock formations in **Antelope Canyon** (visitarizona.com) and **Horseshoe Bend** (horseshoebend.com).

- **Cape Cod, Massachusetts,** has all the beach you want with almost 600 miles of coastline. You can explore **Cape Cod National Seashore** (nps.gov/caco), go mountain biking, walk or bike the 25-mile **Cape Cod Rail Trail** (capecodbikeguide.com/railtrail.asp), visit historic sites, and eat all the homemade ice cream and fresh seafood you want.

THE SETTING-UP-CAMP CHECKLIST

Are you a happy and helpful camper? Check off what you helped with while setting up camp!

- ☐ Found our campsite
- ☐ Set up the tent or hooked up the RV
- ☐ Found a power source
- ☐ Set up chairs
- ☐ Helped with a meal
- ☐ Washed a dish
- ☐ Collected firewood
- ☐ Unpacked supplies
- ☐ Set up a sleeping bag
- ☐ Made a fire
- ☐ Set up a trash bag
- ☐ Set the picnic table

A MAINE KID SAYS:
"Bring some warm clothes with you, even in summer. At night you may want some sweats to hang out in if you are camping."
—Anna, 12

DID YOU KNOW?

You can find tents that will fit 4 to 12 people—and your pet too. Some even have room dividers and welcome mats.

CAMPSITE CROSSWORD

Across

1) Corn chips or anything else dry and crinkly can work in a pinch.

2) The best campsite neighbors are . . .

3) A home on wheels that you brought from home.

Down

4) Keeps things cool and fights dehydration.

5) A must-have for dog walking.

6) If you don't have a flashlight, grab a . . .

7) The first thing you need to make a campfire.

See page 120 for the answers!

4

What's Cooking?

Have you ever made a tinfoil dinner?

You can make it with fish (that you caught!), hamburger, chicken, or all veggies. And this is something you can (mostly) do yourself with your brothers and sisters while your parents take a break!

You'll need some potatoes, carrots, and onions. Add whatever you have on hand or have picked up at the farmers' market—corn, green beans, red peppers. You can even add fruit (lemon or orange with the fish or chicken, pineapple, or peach). Add the seasoning you like—instant onion soup mix, maybe, garlic, salt, and pepper . . . a dash of olive oil and, if you like spicy food, a few drops of hot sauce, or ketchup. (Soy sauce works on chicken!)

Build your mixture inside a big enough piece of aluminum foil to fold inside. Rub butter or oil on the foil and then place the food you want to cook on top. If you are cooking on a grill or a campfire, use heavy-duty foil or two layers. Wrap the food well in the foil so that it won't fall apart when you take it off the grill or out of the fire. Cook for about 40 minutes.

Presto! A camping dinner that is guaranteed to be a hit with everyone. Good job!

What other recipes would you like to help make?

There are plenty of websites that will help you come up with ideas, including the KOA library (koa.com/camping-recipes).

A KOA MONTANA
CAMPING KID SAYS:
"The best part of an RV trip is waking up to the fresh smell of breakfast. My favorite meal when we are camping is a big breakfast with eggs, bacon, and potatoes."
—Adalyn, 10

It's a good idea to choose some recipes before the trip so you have the right ingredients on hand. You can help plan the menus, make a shopping list, and get groceries. What you choose, of course, will be different if you have an RV with a fridge and stove, are car camping with just a cooler, or backpacking and having to carry your food with you.

Campgrounds often have stores where you can find what you've forgotten or something you really want. In fact, every KOA campground has a camp store. But they aren't like big supermarkets. That's why it's a good idea to be prepared in advance!

Maybe you and your brothers and sisters can take turns planning meals for the trip. Maybe you can come up with a new dish no one has tried.

Campgrounds are very friendly places. If you make some new friends, ask your parents if you can invite them to your fire and roast s'mores together. If you're lucky, snap a picture with your campfire friends and share it online. Don't forget to use #KOAcamping!

"Some Mores," Please!

No one knows for sure who invented the s'more. However, the first published recipe for "some mores" was in the 1927 Girl Scout Handbook—roasted marshmallows with chocolate bars and graham crackers around a campfire. Today you are limited only by what you like. Here are some ideas for campfire marshmallows:

- Instead of graham crackers, use different kinds of cookies, such as oatmeal cookies or sugar cookies.

- Instead of a chocolate bar use a peanut butter cup, Nutella, a Peppermint Patty, or a caramel chocolate bar. Not using chocolate is fine too!

A MAINE KID SAYS:
"Campfires, hot dogs, fresh fish . . . s'mores. Food cooked on the fire always tastes so good!"
—Aaron, 12

- Also add jam, fresh banana, peanut butter, and anything else you can think of.

DID YOU KNOW?

People have been roasting marshmallows since 2000 BCE. But ancient Egyptians reserved the treat—made from the sap of the marshmallow plant and a honey-based candy recipe—for the pharaohs. French candy makers were the first to make the kind we have today by whipping the marshmallow sap with egg whites and sugar

A Recipe That Went Viral

Campfire éclairs are easy to make and delicious. No wonder the recipe from the KOA blog (koa.com/blog) went viral and was shared by millions.

You will need:

Ingredients

1-inch dowels or broom handles

Heavy-duty aluminum foil

Cooking spray

1 can refrigerated crescent rolls

Premade chocolate and
    vanilla pudding cups

Whipped cream

Chocolate hazelnut spread

Directions

1. Wrap dowels with aluminum foil and coat with cooking spray.

2. Open can of rolls and separate into rectangles, pressing together dough where it is scored into three triangles. Wrap each dowel with one rectangle.

3. Hold over campfire, turning occasionally, until dough has turned golden brown and puffy.

4. Remove from heat, cool slightly, and fill with pudding and whipped cream. Top with chocolate hazelnut spread and dig in!

Food Fest!

Especially in summer and fall, you'll likely find state fairs and food and harvest festivals near where you are camping. Just check that they are scheduled, as they were canceled in 2020. (They all were closed during the pandemic, and there's no telling if they will be back in 2021.) They have lots of music, games, and plenty of yummy tastes. Here are a few:

- **Piscataquis County, Maine,** celebrates the state's favorite dessert at the **Maine Whoopie Pie Festival** (mainewhoopiepiefestival .com) in June. For the uninitiated, it's two big cookies with different kinds of cream filling.

- **Morton, Illinois,** is home to the **Morton Pumpkin Festival** (mortonpumpkinfestival.org), the state's premier family festival, offering a Big Wheel race, boxcar derby, pumpkin bike tour, and more.

- **Gettysburg, Pennsylvania,** celebrates all things apple during the first two weekends in October at their **National Apple Harvest Festival** (appleharvest.com). This festival in the heart of Pennsylvania apple country offers lots of crafts, a Kid Country Barn, petting zoo, puppet show, and plenty of orchards nearby to pick your own bushel.

- **Half Moon Bay, California,** celebrates being "the Pumpkin Capital of the World" with the **Half Moon Bay Art and Pumpkin Festival** (pumpkinfest.miramarevents.com). There are experts carving giant pumpkins, the world's biggest pumpkin sculpture, costume contests, and, of course, the chance to pick your own pumpkin.

DID YOU KNOW?

The largest pumpkins can weigh more than 2,500 pounds. There are contests every year around the country for the largest pumpkin.

What's for Lunch?

Help your parents figure out what to have in the cooler for lunch. Suggest something different with products made where you are visiting! Maybe you can try Hatch Chili Salsa in New Mexico, Cape Cod Potato Chips in Massachusetts, bread from a local bakery, or homemade chocolate from a local shop. Pick up:

- locally made tortillas (great with honey and peanut butter!)

- carrots and other veggies with pita bread and hummus

- local cheese, salami, and crackers

- fruits that won't get crushed, such as apples, frozen grapes, and clementines

- treats for dessert

{ **What's Cool?** Inventing your own personal version of GORP (Good Old Raisins and Peanuts). Add anything you like, including pretzels, M&M's, other dried fruits, or granola. What would you add?

TELL THE ADULTS: A FOOD ADVENTURE!

Everything always tastes better when you are camping—most of the time anyway. That's why it's a great time to make your outdoor adventure a food adventure too. You can buy what's in season, encourage the kids to chat up local farmers at farmers' markets and maybe have them sample a kind of vegetable or fruit they may not have at home. Look for locally made brands at the market. The best camping food is made on the grill or by the fire. Try breakfast, lunch, and dinner for one day all at your site.

What's Cool? Going to a local farmers' market near where you are camping. Especially in summer, you can find one nearly every week. Search for one nearby at www.ams.usda.gov/market-news/local-regional-food.

WHAT DID YOU EAT TODAY?

Did you try one of the yummy recipes in this chapter? Did you try something new today? Draw what you ate!

A KOA UTAH
CAMPING KID SAYS:
"Spend as much time with your family as you can. You will see how much fun that is!"
—Vivian, 12, Vernal/ Dinosaurland KOA

5
National Parks
for All Seasons

Ready to learn something new?

Many national parks have a junior ranger program, a really fun way to explore! Ask park staff when you arrive, or ask at your campground before you head out

for the day. Junior ranger guide booklets are available at the visitor centers. Some of the big parks even have different offerings for different ages. Complete the activities while you explore the park—maybe identify different birds, or kinds of rocks, animals, or trees you have seen. When you are finished, stop by the visitor center and talk to a ranger, who will swear you in and give you your badge.

Some kids like to put all their badges on a backpack or special vest.

DID YOU KNOW?

President Theodore Roosevelt was the conservationist in chief. After he became president in 1901, he did all he could to protect public lands and wildlife by creating the US Forest Service, establishing 150 national forests, 51 federal bird reserves, 4 national game preserves, 5 national parks, and 18 national monuments.

STATE
— PARK —

Many families camp in and around national parks, often visiting several on one trip. You can make the most of your visit if you take a virtual tour first. Just visit nps.gov and search for the parks you plan to visit. There is also a **Kids in Parks** site (nps.gov/kids).

Your first stop when you arrive at a national park should be a visitor center. You'll want to get a map (remember you may not have Wi-Fi in a big national park) and talk to one of the rangers. See what family activities will be going on while you are there. Ask the ranger to suggest hikes, bike rides, and other activities you might like. See if there are explorer backpacks you can borrow.

A KOA CALIFORNIA CAMPING KID SAYS:
"I've been to Yellowstone and Grand Teton National Park. Grand Teton was my favorite because we river rafted on the Snake River."
—Layla, 12

When you visit a national park or camp there, it's really important to follow the rules. They are meant to keep you safe and protect the environment all around you and the creatures who call the park home. Make sure you:

- Only hike or bike on designated paths and trails.

- Put trash in trash cans and recycling in bins.

- Don't take anything, not even a rock. Can you imagine if each of the more than three million visitors to the Grand Canyon each year took a rock as a souvenir?

- Give people room to pass you if they are hiking or biking faster than you are.

- If you are in a place where dogs are permitted, make sure yours is leashed and you clean up after it.

- Respect wildlife and keep your distance at all times.

That's not too hard, right?

> **A COLORADO KID SAYS:**
> "There is lots of great wildlife at Rocky Mountain National Park. Last time, we saw a moose!"
> —Abel, 12

DID YOU KNOW?

The Grizzly Giant in Yosemite National Park (nps.gov/yose) is the oldest redwood tree—it's between 1,900 and 2,400 years old. You'll find it in the park's Mariposa Grove along with other giant trees.

Wildlife Smarts

National parks are great places to see wildlife—everything from a huge elk to a tiny hummingbird to whales and sea creatures in tide pools, depending on where you are. The national park rangers at the visitor centers can give you an idea of when—and where—you can see wildlife safely.

Be respectful. Remember, you are visiting their home:

- Keep your distance. You never want to approach wildlife.

- Do not feed wildlife. They won't survive if they become dependent on human food.

- Explore tide pools at low tide and don't take any creature (such as a sea star) with you.

- Bring a pocket guide or use an app on your phone to identify what you are seeing.

- Join a ranger-led group to learn more.

AN OKLAHOMA KID SAYS:
"I saw so many animals in Yellowstone—a ton of elk and even a baby moose."
—Claire, 13

DON'T FEED THE WILDLIFE!

National Park Rangers

See the big Smoky the Bear hat?

National park rangers wear them. You might meet a ranger in the visitor center or a campfire program. Some do special programs for kids and families.

They can tell you about an especially fun hike or a place to see a beaver dam. They help when you get hurt and when there are big crowds. Some may work on fire crews and others on the parks' websites. Many are scientists—geologists and biologists, for example.

Some rangers work in big cities at national monuments like the Lincoln Memorial in Washington, DC. Many have studied something like forestry or environmental science in college.

Today, no matter what their assignment, they are all stewards for the national parks. Say thank you when you meet them!

A MONTANA KID SAYS:
"There aren't any distractions when you are camping and it's really nice to enjoy what's all around you."
—Kennedy, 10

What's Cool? A Full Moon Ranger Walk, where you can learn about nocturnal animals in a national park.

Skip the Crowds

There are 62 national parks in the US and hundreds more national park sites—historic monuments, national recreation areas, battlefields, and memorials among them. Some get millions of visitors and can be so crowded it's hard to find a parking place in the summer; others get far fewer visitors but offer just as much to see and do. Here are a few less crowded, but equally awesome, parks.

The Great Sand Dunes National Park (nps.gov/grsa) in Mosca, Colorado, has the tallest sand dunes in the country. Here's the place to go sand surfing and sand sledding!

You have to take a boat to get to **The Channel Islands National Park** (nps.gov/chis) in Ventura, California. Once you are there, you can camp, snorkel, and kayak. See how many different birds you can find!

Voyageurs National Park (nps.gov/voya) in International Falls, Minnesota, is close to the Canadian border. You can go fishing or kayaking, canoe, camp, or stargaze.

Congaree National Park (nps.gov/cong) in Hopkins, South Carolina, is a great place for a hike whether you want to head into the backcountry, to a lake through an old-growth forest, or to the Congaree River.

North Cascades National Park (nps.gov/noca) in the state of Washington has plenty of biking, hiking, and fishing! There's even the chance to take a rafting trip down a river.

DID YOU KNOW?

More than 12 million people visit Great Smoky Mountains National Park (nps.gov/grsm) every year. It's the most-visited national park in the country, but many visitors just drive through without getting out of their cars. They're called "windshield visitors."

TELL THE ADULTS: AMERICA THE BEAUTIFUL

A tip: National parks often have areas on their websites for teachers that provide lots of information and great ideas for family visits too.

If you plan to visit more than one national park in a year, the National Parks and Federal Recreational Lands Pass (usgs.gov/pass) gives you and your family access to more than 2,000 federal recreation sites.

Passes are free for those with disabilities and members of the military and their families and $80 for all others. You can buy passes at the park or online.

If you are traveling with seniors, those aged 62 and older can get an Annual Senior Pass ($20) or a Lifetime Senior Pass ($80). These passes cover everyone in the car and can also be used for discounts on campsites, tours, and more.

Fourth graders and their families can get into national parks free through the Every Kid in a Park program (everykid inapark.gov/get-your-pass/fourth-grader). Print the paper pass and exchange it for the official pass at national parks that charge entrance fees.

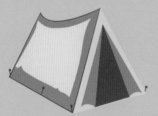

What's Cool? Camping under the stars in a national park or in a KOA campground next to one. Can you see the Milky Way? It might look like a faint cloud, but it's really the light from millions and millions of stars far away. Many national parks offer night sky programs and are certified by the International Dark Sky Association (darksky.org).

MATCH THE NATIONAL PARK TO THE STATE

There are national parks in so many different states! Can you match the national parks below to the state that they are in?

Acadia National Park   Grand Canyon National Park
Yosemite National Park   Yellowstone National Park
Glacier National Park   Rocky Mountain National Park
Big Bend National Park   Shenandoah National Park
Olympic National Park   Cuyahoga Valley National Park

See page 120 for the answers!

6

Camping Greener

Camping is a great way to get closer

to nature. Finding environmentally friendly ways to do things helps protect the plants and animals that call our campgrounds home year-round, and to protect nature for the next visitors and future generations. How can you go green on your camping trip? Try to produce less trash by bringing reusable plates, cups, and utensils. Clean up after your activities to leave nature as you found it.

Get a special camping water bottle! Not a disposable one—a reusable one. It will become a souvenir once you put some stickers from where you've been on it. If you are hiking a lot on your camping trip, you may want to use a backpack that has a flexible, plastic "bladder" built in for water. You don't need to carry a separate water bottle, and the hose lets you drink hands-free. Nice!

Not only is that more convenient, but you'll be helping the planet by creating less trash.

DID YOU KNOW?

Every water bottle with a built-in water purifier bought from **LifeStraw** (lifestraw.com) helps provides kids safe water to drink at their schools.

Just don't fill up your water bottle from a stream unless you know the water is safe to drink. It can make you sick. If you are going to be in the wilderness, ask your parents about getting a water bottle that has a built-in water purifier.

You can do your part wherever you are to protect the land and all the creatures that live there. That's why national parks were first created.

Zoos, aquariums, and animal rescue centers are also great places to learn about threatened and endangered animals. They do a lot to help with conservation projects around the world. You might be able to "adopt" an animal you really like to help support those projects.

In case you are wondering, a species that is in danger of extinction is endangered; a threatened species is one that is likely to become endangered. Some animals, such as Steller sea lions, gray wolves, and giant pandas, are no longer endangered because of conservation efforts around the world.

There are a lot of little things you can do to camp greener. You can:

- Use public shuttles or buses from the campground rather than taking your car or RV, though you may need reservations in advance.

- Always turn off the lights after you use campground bathrooms or when you are not in the RV.

- Take shorter showers!

- Pack your snacks and lunches in reusable bags or containers.

- Pay attention to where your food comes from! Foods that are grown and produced locally won't use nearly as much energy to get to a store.

- "Pack it in, pack it out." Always make sure to bring any trash you create with you when you leave.

It's a lot easier than you thought!

DID YOU KNOW?

Every minute, a garbage truck of plastic is dumped into our oceans. Many marine animals can't tell the difference between plastic and food, and those who eat plastic often get sick and may die.

{ **What's Cool?** Upcycling! Upcycling is the process of taking an unused or needed item and turning it into something wonderful. For instance, you can take a used glass jar and paint it to create a coin bank or vase. Learn how to upcycle at upcyclethat.com.

PICK UP AMERICA

Wherever you are in the wilderness or outdoors, it's your responsibility to leave a place the way you found it—or better.

You can do your part to keep the shared spaces we love the way they were meant to be—clean and pristine—by participating in **Pick Up America** (pickupamerica.com), a program where campers, RVers, and outdoor enthusiasts are asked to set a positive example by pledging to pick up trash wherever they find it. You can pledge 1 bag or 10, every bit helps. Pick up bags at:

- National and state parks
- Biking/hiking trails
- Rest stops
- Picnic areas
- Local parks
- Roadsides (where it's safe)
- Your favorite outdoor spot

A KOA CALIFORNIA CAMPING KID SAYS:
"The best thing you can do to help the environment when you are camping is to clean up after yourself."
—Tyler, 14

Bring a small trash bag when you are hiking, and if you see litter that is not dangerous to touch, pick it up.

Make your pledge to help Pick Up America and share your quest for a cleaner world using #PickUpAmerica.

WHAT DID THAT BIRD SAY?

When you are camping and visiting wilderness areas, you will see—and hear—a lot of birds. Stop, look, and listen! How many different birds have you seen?

Kids like to go birding across the country, from Acadia National Park off the east coast of Maine to the California seashore. At the **Aspen Center for Environmental Studies** (aspennature.org) in Colorado, you can climb up to get a bird's-eye view and meet the resident rescued raptors who can no longer live in the wild. **Point Reyes National Seashore** (nps.gov/pore) in California has nearly 490 different species—that's more than half of all the species of birds in North America, and more than in any other national park. Have you ever seen a northern spotted owl? Here, you might!

A TENNESSEE KID SAYS: "Leave wildlife alone and don't feed the animals in national parks!" —Nevaeh, 10

There are lots of fun apps you can try on your phone if you have one. The free **Audubon Bird Guide** app (apple.com/us/developer/national-audubon-society/id1007642225) can help you identify more than 800 North American birds, the **iBird Pro Guide to Birds** (ibird.com) identifies birds from your photos, and the free **Song Sleuth** app from the App Store helps you record and identify bird calls.

Bring binoculars and a small notebook so you can write down which bird species you see. You may be able to get a guide to birds of the region you are visiting.

Now all you need to do is slow down, watch, and listen.

CITIZEN SCIENTIST: WHAT KIDS CAN DO

Do you like science experiments? You can help scientists by collecting data for them. See if a national or state park near where you are camping has a **Citizen Science Program** (citizenscience.gov) for kids.

You can also check out:

Frog Watch USA (aza.org/frogwatch), a project of the Association of Zoos and Aquariums that allows you to report data on the calls of local frogs and toads.

Project Squirrel (projectsquirrel.org) from the University of Chicago wants to know where you see squirrels and what they are doing.

iNaturalist (inaturalist.org) offers a way to upload your observations and photographs of plants, animals, and other organisms. It's a joint program from the California Academy of Sciences and the National Geographic Society.

Globe at Night (globeatnight.org), a program that documents light pollution. How visible are the constellations?

{ What's Cool? The **Animal Care Center** at Busch Gardens Tampa Bay (buschgardens.com/tampa), where you can watch and even take part in the animal care. The Animal Care Center is also home to the hit Emmy-nominated TV series *The Wildlife Docs*.

TELL THE ADULTS: CAMPING GREENER

Kampgrounds of America (KOA) has been sponsoring green initiatives for the past decade to encourage campgrounds and campers to be good stewards of the environment. Look for the **Kamp Green**® logo on campground web pages designating environmentally friendly features like solar shade structures, rainwater collectors, vegetable gardens, and wind turbines.

Here are some ways your family can camp greener:

- Keep windows and doors closed in the RV when the AC is on.

- Use the campground's recycling container or set up your own.

- Don't burn or bury trash.

- Pack food in reusable containers.

- Use biodegradable soaps, shampoos, and detergents.

DID YOU KNOW?

Many restaurants are now banning plastic straws. That's because most end up in the ocean polluting the water and hurting animals. You can help seabirds, turtles, and other marine creatures simply by not using plastic straws (#strawlessocean).

CAMPING GREEN WORD SCRAMBLE

You learned a lot about how to be friendly to the environment while camping. Now that you're an expert "green camper," unscramble some of the words and terms below!

OIBGDEARDBAEL __ __ __ __ __ __ __ __ __ __ __ __ __

EAVEL ON ARTCE __ __ __ __ __ __ __ __ __ __ __ __

CLEYCRE __ __ __ __ __ __ __

APKC NI CKAP TOU

__ __ __ __ __ __ __ __ __ __ __ __ __

BLEUSARE __ __ __ __ __ __ __ __

VATSERIONCNO __ __ __ __ __ __ __ __ __ __ __ __

TSOSYEMEC __ __ __ __ __ __ __ __ __

ATHIATB __ __ __ __ __ __ __

A MAINE KID SAYS:
"In [national parks] take only pictures and leave only footprints."
—Adam, 11

See page 121 for the answers!

7

What's in Your Backpack: Hiking and Biking Smarts

Ready to go for a ride?

Lots of kids—and their parents—bring bikes on camping trips because there are so many places for rides—national and state parks, rail trails that once were for trains, on mountains, and around campgrounds.

A lot of families like to hike on camping trips too. Just make sure you don't get separated on the trail!

You can ask at the campground for suggestions of hikes. National Park rangers also will have good ideas. Just choose a hike that won't be too hard for anyone in your group. Have you ever climbed to the top of a mountain? Through a creek bed? Make sure to take a picture when you get to the end of the trail!

Check out peopleforbikes.org to browse where to ride by state.

DID YOU KNOW?

There are apps to help you identify what you are seeing while you hike—like the free Audubon Bird Guide app (audubon.org/app) or a free **Wildflower Search** app for the state where you are (wildflowersearch.org).

Have you ever been mountain biking? That's when you ride off the road with special bikes meant for rough terrain. You'll find a lot of mountain bike trails (and places to rent mountain bikes) at ski resorts in the summer and fall. You can take a ski lift up with your bike and ride a trail down.

You can also mountain bike on backcountry roads. Some national parks, like **Acadia National Park** in Maine (nps.gov/acad), are known for biking—there are no motorized vehicles allowed on Acadia's famous Carriage Roads—45 miles! But you'll have to share them with people on horseback!

Wherever you go biking, make sure to wear a helmet that fits snugly. And if you are mountain biking, you'll want protective gear for your elbows and knees too as well as plenty of water and high-energy snacks. (Biking takes a lot of energy!)

A COLORADO KID SAYS:
"It's really fun to go biking along the bike trails in the mountains. I really love when you get to bike next to a river!"
—Olivia, 10

It's important to stay safe! Here are some guidelines:

- Before you set out, make sure the brakes and gearshifts work.

- If you are renting a bike, take a quick spin on it to get used to it before starting your ride.

- Don't wear loose clothing that can get caught in bike chains.

- Wear bright colors and use lights when needed.

- Stay to the right when traveling and pass on the left.

- Move to the side of the road when you are stopped.

- Yield to hikers and walkers.

What are you waiting for?

A KOA MONTANA KID SAYS:
"I always have bear spray, bug spray, a hydroflask, and a rope with a hook in case I need to climb up on a rock. . . . Digging up rocks is my favorite thing to do on an RV road trip."
—Hudson, 7

What's in Your Pack?

Maybe the weather changes. Maybe you scratch your knee. Here's what you want to have in your backpack when you are hiking:

- an extra layer, like a fleece

- sunglasses

- a hat

- a trail map (you can download one on your phone if you don't have a paper one)

- a spare pair of non-cotton socks (in case your shoes get soaked);

- wet wipes

- a plastic trash bag (you can line your pack with an extra one in case it rains)

- flashlight and extra batteries

- rain gear

- a portable charger for your phone

- first aid kit, or at least some Band-Aids and antiseptic

- a magnifying glass (great to get a close-up view of something on the trail!)

- binoculars (for looking at birds and wildlife)

- water and healthy snacks or lunch if you are going on an all-day hike

- a small notebook and pen (to write down what birds, flowers, and trees you see)

- face mask (until the COVID-19 pandemic is over)

A MAINE KID SAYS:
"The essentials for hiking are a water bottle, snacks, and lunch."
—Zoey, 11

TELL THE ADULTS: HIKING SAFETY

Every year people get hurt and lost while hiking—adults as well as kids. You have to be prepared! Keep in mind:

- Your cell phone may not be your friend if there is no service.

- Don't attempt a hike that is too difficult for any one member of the group.

- Remind the kids what they should do if they get separated— "hug a tree," and wait for you to return for them.

You can get a prepackaged first aid kit or make a DIY kit. Here is what REI suggests you have in yours:

- assorted adhesive bandages,

- gauze pads and nonstick sterile pads,

- medical adhesive tape,

- tube of antibiotic cream,

A KOA CALIFORNIA KID SAYS:
"Don't forget bug spray!"
—Genesis, 10

- anti-itch cream for bites,

- antihistamine to treat allergic reactions and injectable epinephrine if someone is severely allergic,

- ibuprofen and an antidiarrheal,

- aspirin,

- oral rehydration salts,

- 2 to 3 antiseptic wipes,

- 2 to 3 butterfly bandages,

- fine-point tweezers for splinters or thorns,

- safety pins,

- a first aid manual (you can download one to your phone from the American Red Cross, among other places).

What's Cool? Having a special "surprise" treat in your pack to share when everyone is tired—trail mix, fruit, and jerky are great options.

Hiking Smarts

Wherever you are camping, you will find great hikes nearby. Just be careful to:

- Stay on established trails at all times.

- Keep pace with your group. Lagging behind or rushing ahead is dangerous.

- Carry a whistle. (You can blow it to alert rangers or other adults if you get in trouble. Always stay put if you get separated.)

- Keep hydrated, carry water, and drink it. Your body needs water more than anything.

- Know your environment. If bears are in the area, you'll need bear spray, and, if there are streams through the trails, you might want water shoes.

{ **What's Cool?** The AllTrails free app that can help you find the perfect hike or bike ride based on length, difficulty, dog-friendly status, and where you are (alltrails.com/mobile).

A Super Trail

What's the farthest you can hike? How about 2,180 miles?

Every year, some 2,000 people try to hike the **Appalachian Trail** (appalachiantrail.org) that winds through 14 states—North Carolina, Tennessee, Virginia, West Virginia, Maryland, Pennsylvania, New Jersey, New York, Connecticut, Massachusetts, Vermont, and New Hampshire. It starts in Georgia and ends in Maine. You might be able to hike a small part of it.

Hikers stay in rustic shelters along the trail, carrying food in heavy packs. Volunteers work along the way to keep the trail maintained.

It takes about six months to hike the entire trail, starting in Georgia in the spring and ending in Maine in the fall, but only one in four people who start actually finish.

Along the way, hikers adopt nicknames like "Crumb-snatcher" or "Thunder Chicken." Do you have a trail nickname?

DID YOU KNOW?

There are 23,000 miles of rail trails across the country—multipurpose public paths created from former railroad corridors. They are great places to bike, inline skate, and walk. They are also a great way for those in a wheelchair to enjoy the outdoors. Check out railstotrails.org to see if there's one near you.

GET BACK TO CAMP

After a long day of hiking and biking all around, can you find your way back to camp? Stay safe and be careful of taking a wrong turn!

See page 121 for the answer!

ITS A WORD SAFARI!

Can you find all ten phrases?

SUNGLASSES	WATER	MAP
FLASHLIGHT	JACKET	CAMERA
BUG SPRAY	TISSUES	BAG
TRIP		

```
Q  O  Y  V  J  X  Q  Q  A  E
W  N  Y  W  T  E  Y  V  M  W
F  L  A  S  H  L  I  G  H  T
C  K  G  V  W  Q  I  K  D  T
F  U  J  G  B  P  X  V  L  I
Z  R  R  N  Z  K  S  Z  C  S
Y  A  G  Z  G  H  V  E  T  S
F  B  U  G  S  P  R  A  Y  U
A  H  K  W  C  Q  T  I  F  E
X  J  Z  U  Y  K  N  N  R  S
S  L  K  Z  L  E  Y  Y  N  W
G  B  O  T  F  P  P  I  G  J
S  U  N  G  L  A  S  S  E  S
J  R  X  K  W  T  B  K  Y  X
B  J  H  Z  T  E  C  P  T  N
C  A  M  E  R  A  D  O  M  W
S  C  L  F  I  B  V  E  S  A
S  K  L  C  P  S  K  G  E  T
H  E  M  H  B  W  Y  B  Q  E
O  T  J  C  A  N  S  G  V  R
P  B  W  G  G  N  M  A  P  C
O  R  V  X  W  U  J  Q  O  W
Z  H  L  J  V  F  O  J  L  C
```

See page 122 for the answers!

8

Water and Campground Fun and Games

River, lake or ocean?

Many families like to camp near water so they can enjoy water sports. There are so many ways to have fun on or near the water—take your pick! You can fish, take a raft or tube down a river, explore in a kayak or canoe, water-ski on a lake, discover tide pools, float leisurely in a pool, or surf in the ocean. Want to stay dry? Build a giant sand sculpture.

If you're lucky, your campground will have a pool. Some Kampgrounds of America (KOA) campgrounds even have splash and wading pool areas designed specifically for the youngest member of your family. The areas can feature shallow wading areas, light stream water showers, and comfortable seating for parents and guardians.

There are even KOAs with waterslides and full water parks. Some offer hot tubs for chilly evenings, so poolside fun can be had in the spring and fall. (Check to see what each campground provides on the campground's KOA.com landing page.)

DID YOU KNOW?

The five Great Lakes—Superior, Huron, Michigan, Ontario, and Erie—make up the largest body of fresh water on Earth. They have been a major source of transportation, migration, trade, and fishing.

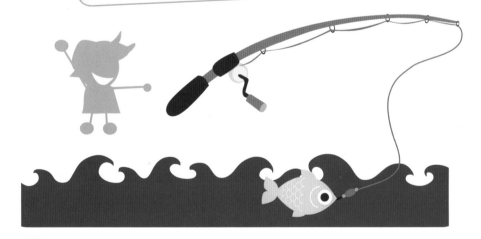

There are also places to camp near ponds, lakes, and beaches! So if you prefer getting a more natural campground water feature you can. The best part of natural water features is the fishing and wildlife that you can see as well, watch for storks, seals, and otters!

Water sports, of course, are one of the best ways to stay cool in the summer while camping. There's no better time to try a new water sport with your family—and maybe your pooch. (Do you have a dog toy that floats so you can play fetch in the water?)

KOA suggests these water sports:

WAKEBOARDING: Think of snowboarding on water. It's easier to get up on a wakeboard than skis. Wakeboarding is especially fun for those who want to try jumping in the boat's wake!

AN ARIZONA KID SAYS:
"You are never too old to make sandcastles!"
—Gabrielle, 13

KNEEBOARDING: You might even get up on your first try! Kneeboarding is a lot easier than waterskiing. You rest your knees on a teardrop-shaped board with a strap over your thighs and you hold on to a towrope.

SURFING: Take a lesson if you are near the ocean. You have to be patient to wait for the right wave, but then you paddle with the wave and ride it back toward shore. So fun! It's also fun to watch the surfers on beaches in southern California, among other places. Huntington Beach is called Surf City USA, in fact. Find more information at surfcityusa.com.

BODYSURFING: Bodysurfing lets you catch a wave without needing a board. But it can be harder to catch that wave.

CANOEING AND KAYAKING: Canoeing and kayaking are great ways to watch wildlife—waterbirds, river otters, and more—even bears snacking on salmon at the shore if you are in Alaska. Pack a picnic!

A KOA WASHINGTON CAMPING KID SAYS:
"Go tubing! There are some rapids that are pretty fun!"
—Kiera, 8, Winthrop/ N. Cascades KOA

{ What's Cool? Swimming in a hot springs pool like in Glenwood Springs, Colorado (hotspringspool.com), home to the world's largest hot springs pool.

STANDUP PADDLEBOARDING: You'll be surprised how stable the board is as you stand up and paddle across a lake, in the ocean, or on a river. Some people standup paddleboard through rapids on white water raft trips!

DID YOU KNOW?

When you are waterskiing and drop a ski (on purpose), that's called slaloming. It's not easy! Think of riding your bike without training wheels the first time.

WINDSURFING: Think of sailing back and forth on your own. Because winds and water are always changing, windsurfing never gets boring! A lot of people like to watch the windsurfers in Hood River, Oregon (visithoodriver.com), which is considered the windsurfing capital of the world. You'll find a lot of windsurfers in many other places as well, from South Padre Island, Texas, to San Francisco, California, to Cape Hatteras, North Carolina. (Hint: there are KOAs near all of these.)

How many new water sports can you try on one camping trip?

Fishing 101

There's a reason they call it fishing, not catching. Whether you are fishing in a river, a lake, or even the ocean, there aren't guarantees you'll catch dinner. You are guaranteed to have fun! Each type of fishing requires its own skills and equipment. You can fish in a kayak, canoe, or from shore. Remind your parents to get a fishing license. Here are a few fishing tips from the experts:

- Fish early in the morning or in the evening.

- Don't wear bright colors. You don't want the fish to see you.

- Don't let your shadow fall on the water because you can spook the fish!

- Don't stay in one place too long. Fish a spot for a little while and then move on.

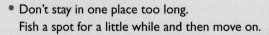

A KOA MONTANA CAMPING KID SAYS:
"My favorite thing to do around water is playing on a rope swing and swimming."
—Hudson, 7

What's a Tide Pool?

Tide pools are rocky pockets by the shore that hold water when the tide goes out. Some are large and others very small. They're home to an entire community of sea life—anemones, sponges, worms, snails, sea slugs, mussels, crabs, starfish, and sea urchins.

Low tide is the best time to explore these pools. If you're lucky, you might see an octopus!

You'll find tide pools everywhere from Cannon Beach, Oregon, to Laguna Beach, California. Check out **Bahia Honda State Park** (floridastateparks.org/BahiaHonda) in Florida and **Acadia National Park** (nps.gov/acad) in Maine, among other places. You'll also find tide pool touch tanks at many aquariums around the country.

Remember, these creatures are fragile! Even turning over a rock can hurt a tiny animal not used to the sun. Remember, you shouldn't take anything home! Empty seashells might provide a home for some creature later.

A CALIFORNIA KID SAYS:
"I've learned a lot from tide pools about creatures I never knew about!"
—Andi, 13

Lifeguards

You'll see them patrolling beaches, pools, and water parks all around the country.

It's a hard job! They make sure people are following the rules, administer first aid, and rescue those who need help. A lot of high school and college students take courses from the American Red Cross to become certified lifeguards. The LA County Lifeguards in California work for a division of the Los Angeles County Fire Department. They are some of the most highly trained lifeguards in the world.

Here are some things you can do to help lifeguards do their job—and keep yourself safe:

- Ask lifeguards about surf conditions before you go in the water.

- Never dive if you don't know how deep the water is.

- Avoid swimming near a storm drain outlet.

- Stay calm if you get pulled by a rip current. Try to swim at an angle toward shore and, if you can, call for help.

DID YOU KNOW?

Even if it's cloudy outside, you can get sunburn. That's why you always need to wear sunscreen. And even if it is waterproof, you should reapply every few hours, the experts say.

TELL THE ADULTS: WATER SAFETY

It's easy to let down your guard when you are relaxing around the pool or on the beach. Don't! Drownings happen in seconds—and can happen silently. The American Red Cross has developed a free swim app (redcross.org/get-help/how-to-prepare-for-emergencies/mobile-apps) to promote water safety, including games. Here's how to make your water fun safer:

- Designate one adult to be a "water watcher" for a period of time (30 minutes), even if there are lifeguards on duty.

- Stay within "touching distance" of preschoolers and toddlers around and in the water.

- Make it a rule that older kids swim with a buddy.

- Don't rely on water wings or other inflatable toys to keep kids safe.

- When boating, insist everyone wear Coast Guard–approved life jackets.

What's Cool? White water rafting or tubing on a river.

Campground Fun and Games

Every KOA campground offers lots of ways to play outdoors. Here are some of the fun activities you might find:

- **Jumping Pillows:** These are giant outdoor pillows built into the ground for loads of fun. Adults and kids alike can have a bounce and enjoy the sunny weather.

- **Mini-golf:** Mini-golf is a fun way for the family to enjoy the campground. Many KOAs have a mini-golf course, some with big obstacles like waterfalls!

- **Bikes:** There are several kinds of bikes to try, including banana bikes, tandem bikes, electric bikes, and regular bikes. You can rent these for an hour or all day.

- **Water Fun:** Splash pads, waterslides, and even water parks are at many KOAs. Almost every one of them has a pool.

- **Zip Lining:** Zip lining is available at some KOAs. It is supervised, of course! Enjoy flying through the trees, over water, and over the campground.

- **Campground Activity Parks:** These are the place for family fun—and to make new friends—playing games like cornhole, ladder ball, horseshoes, and even giant checkers!

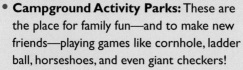

DID YOU KNOW?

People in Polynesia and South America have used surfboards for fishing since prehistoric times.

SECRET DECODER

Have you ever created a secret code with your friends? See if you can figure out the following words using the code below.

A=X	E=V	I=T	M=L	Q=J	U=H	Y=A
B=Y	F=W	J=O	N=M	R=K	V=C	Z=B
C=Z	G=R	K=P	O=N	S=F	W=D	
D=U	H=S	L=Q	P=I	T=G	X=E	

FPOWHDGSPOT

___ ___ ___ ___ ___ ___ ___ ___ ___ ___

VYOJXPOT

___ ___ ___ ___ ___ ___ ___

RYBYR

___ ___ ___ ___ ___

KYWWMXZJYGW

___ ___ ___ ___ ___ ___ ___ ___ ___ ___

See page 122 for the answers!

9
What Do You See?

Wildflowers come in so many colors.

They are purple and blue, yellow, green, red, pink, and orange.

Being outdoors on foot, bikes, or horseback is a great time to slow down and look around. Bring your phone or camera, a sketch pad, and a magnifying glass, and focus on what you see around you—trees, flowers, different kinds of rocks, animal tracks, and of course animals. Got binoculars? **You just don't want to get close to any animal—big or small.**

If you are near a city, botanic gardens can be great places to learn about the flowers and plants that grow in that part of the country and that you are likely to see when you are camping and hiking. Some have special areas for kids, such as the Mordecai Children's Garden at the **Denver Botanic Gardens** (botanicgardens.org/york-street/mordecai-childrens-garden), the Children's Garden at the **US Botanic Garden** (https://m.usbg.gov/kids-are-welcome-us-botanic-garden) in Washington, DC, or the special Bean Sprouts Family Days at the **San Francisco Botanical Garden** (sfbg.org/family-community) in Golden Gate Park, San Francisco.

DID YOU KNOW?

Tiny Crested Butte, Colorado, is called the wildflower capital because you can see so many wildflowers there. There's even a wildflower festival every summer (crestedbuttewildflowerfestival.com).

When wildflowers bloom depends on the weather and the rain. Usually blooms start in March and at higher elevations into the summer. Many people flock to the desert in early spring and the Rocky Mountains later in the summer to see the best blooms.

Some national parks and state parks are famous for the variety of wildflowers they have. In **Great Smoky Mountains National Park** (nps.gov/grsm/learn/nature/wildflowers.htm), there are more than 1,600 different kinds of flowering plants—including 20 different purple flowers. Have you ever seen a spiderwort? It grows to 3 feet tall!

Joshua Tree National Park (nps.gov/jotr) in southern California is famous for its poppies, and **Saguaro National Park** (nps.gov/sagu) in Arizona for its Sonoran Desert flowers. In Montana is **Glacier National Park** (nps.gov/glac), famous for more than a thousand species of wildflowers, including alpine flowers at high altitude.

Keep track of how many different kinds of flowers and trees you see. Can you spy:

- a yellow black-eyed Susan,

- an orange butterfly milkweed,

- a purple long-spurred violet,

- a red Indian paintbrush?

What's your favorite?

Rocks and Roll

How many different colors can you see in the rocks as you are hiking? How many layers? How many shapes?

Geology is the study of the earth, what it is made of, and how it has changed over time. The earth is about 4.6 billion years old.

Those who study rocks, landforms, and the layers of the earth are called geologists. They help us find important minerals, study fuel sources, and investigate causes of earthquakes, floods, and other natural happenings. Check out **Geology 101** from National Geographic (kids.nationalgeographic.com/explore/science/geology-101).

Natural history museums are great places to learn more about rocks in the region you are visiting—and fossils (like from dinosaurs!) that are found there.

Geologists divide rocks into three large groups:

- **Sedimentary rock** looks like a giant layer cake because it's made from layers of mud from an ancient sea. It's also the softest and easiest rock to break.

- **Metamorphic rock** has wavy layers because it was heated and then squeezed.

- **Igneous rock** looks like crystals. This was molten rock that cooled and formed crystals of different colors. It's also the hardest type of rock.

Everyone sees different things when they look at huge rock formations—a witch, a dragon, a dog. What do you see?

DID YOU KNOW?
A group of owls is called a parliament.

How Many Trees and Leaves Can You Name?

LeafSnap is a really good electronic field guide and app that can help you identify trees by using photographs of leaves. It's free! Find it on Google Play or in the App Store.

Have you ever seen a quaking aspen? They really do shake in the wind! If you pick up a red spruce needle, it will feel spiky and roll between your fingers, while balsam fir trees have flat needles.

Be careful what you touch! You want to steer clear of poison ivy, poison oak, and poison sumac. Here's what you need to know:

- Both poison ivy and poison oak have a stem with a larger leaf at the end and two smaller leaves off the sides that are pointy at the tip. That's why people say, "Leaves of three, let them be!"

- You might see greenish-white berries and flowers on poison ivy in the spring and summer.

- Poison ivy leaves will look reddish in the spring, green in summer, and yellow/orange in fall and grow in a vine or a bush, depending on where you are.

- Poison oak leaves have a wavy appearance and are rounded—bright green in spring; yellow, green, or pink in summer; and dark brown in fall.

- Poison sumac stems are generally red and have more leaves in pairs with just one at the end. They are oval, bright orange in spring, dark green in summer, and red orange in fall. It can grow to be 20 feet tall.

{ **What's Cool?** You can identify flowers and plants—even mushrooms and cacti—by snapping a picture on your phone and using a free app like PlantSnap (plantsnap.com) or FlowerChecker (flowerchecker.com).

Horse Smarts

Giddyap! Whether you are camping on the East Coast, West Coast, or in the Rockies, you may have a chance to go horseback riding. Whether you ride at home or have never been on a horse, remember:

- Horses are big, powerful animals. Respect their strength.

- Always approach a horse from the front and never yell at them.

- Make friends with your horse—do you know his or her name?

- Wear boots or shoes with good heels.

- Wear long pants and a hat to protect you from the sun.

- Listen to what the wranglers say. They know the horses best!

- Watch out for low-hanging branches, fallen logs, and streams.

A KOA MONTANA CAMPING KID SAYS:
"A bear, a moose, deer, and elk are my favorite animals that I've seen in the wild."
—Adalyn, 10

{ **What's Cool?** A selfie in a field of wildflowers—or with a giant tree, like a redwood in northern California. Any camping selfie deserves to be shared—share yours using #KOAcamping.

The Best Camping Pictures

How good are your pictures? Kampgrounds of America (KOA) wants to know! Share them on social media with the hashtag #KOACamping and you could have your photo show up on KOA's feed!

Here's how to make yours the best:

- Steady is best! To make sure you take a clear picture, use a tripod or solid surface to stabilize the camera.

- Shoot during "golden hour." The two hours after sunrise and before sunset are the most beautiful light to shoot in. Midday sun is often too harsh.

- Avoid dead-center photos. If your focus in the picture is not in the middle, it creates a more interesting photo.

- Join the fun! Use the timer and selfie mode to add yourself into the picture. It's better with you!

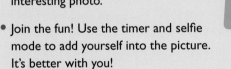

DID YOU KNOW?

A petroglyph is an image carved or scratched into stone and a pictograph is a painting on stone. They both can typically be found in caves or where they have been protected. Some are many thousands of years old. You might see both petroglyphs and pictographs in Horseshoe Canyon, part of Canyonlands National Park (nps.gov/cany) in Utah. Petroglyph National Monument (nps.gov/petr) in Albuquerque, New Mexico, has more than 25,000 individual etchings from the ancestors of the Pueblo.

TELL THE ADULTS: BE PREPARED

Touching poison ivy, poison oak, and poison sumac can derail any camper's fun. A rash might show up immediately or a few days later. Typical symptoms include patches of swollen redness, blisters, and itching. If someone in the family has had a bad allergic reaction in the past, you might want to ask your doctor in advance for a stronger steroid cream than you might be able to get over the counter.

Experts also suggest:

- If you think you have rubbed up against one of these plants, immediately wash with lukewarm, soapy water. If not washed off, the oils can continue to spread. You might want to have on hand a special wash that may lessen the severity of the rash, like Zanfel or Tecnu.

- Make sure you change your clothes when you are finished hiking, and don't wear them again before you wash them. Wash clothing, shoes, or gear that the oil from the plants might have touched. If the oil is on your clothes you can continue to get it on your skin long after your hike.

- Apply calamine lotion or hydrocortisone cream to help with itching; a cool washcloth can also help, as can baking soda.

- Some creams can make it worse; don't use antihistamine, anesthetic, or antibiotic creams.

DID YOU KNOW?
Smoky Mountain black bears spend much of their time in the trees.

NATURE SCAVENGER HUNT

Look carefully around your campsite and the surrounding area for the following creatures, rocks, and plants and check off what you find! Remember: Don't touch wild animals or harmful plants. Appreciate them from a distance!

- ☐ horse
- ☐ wildflower
- ☐ butterfly
- ☐ frog
- ☐ metamorphic rock
- ☐ fossil
- ☐ cactus
- ☐ snake

- ☐ igneous rock
- ☐ sedimentary rock
- ☐ bird
- ☐ deer
- ☐ sapling
- ☐ mushroom
- ☐ lizard
- ☐ animal track

A COLORADO KID SAYS:
"I love looking for birds. My mom and I look online and search by state and feather colors to figure out what birds we see."
—Ben, 8

10

Camping
Fun for All Seasons

Do you have your rain jacket?

Certainly, you don't want to hang out in your tent if it's raining hard. You might not mind, though, if you are staying in an RV or a cabin. Play cards or a board game, maybe. Watch a movie!

But just because it's raining (or snowing if you happen to be in the mountains in the fall) doesn't mean the fun is over. Of course, there is plenty you can do in bad weather—including putting on your boots and jumping in puddles (as long as there is no thunder or lightning!). See if the campground has any special rainy-day activities for kids.

Tell your parents it's the perfect day to go souvenir shopping—and go out for lunch or dinner. Visit a museum. See if you can find one that is kind of strange. Did you know there is even one in Gatlinburg, Tennessee, with 20,000 salt and pepper shakers (thesaltandpeppershakermuseum.com)?

DID YOU KNOW?

President Theodore Roosevelt, who loved the outdoors, refused to shoot a black bear one day in 1902 when he was hunting. After that, stuffed toy bears were made and named for the president. They were the first teddy bears—and still make great souvenirs.

How about visiting a historic landmark or monument? There are many to choose from across the country—houses where famous Americans lived, forts, and more. You can find a state-by-state list on the National Park Service website (nps.gov/subjects/nationalhistoric landmarks/list-of-nhls-by-state.htm).

If you're camping in fall, visit a haunted house—if you dare. The **Haunted House Association** (hauntedattractionassociation.com) will tell you where to find them.

And if the weather isn't too bad, go to a farm or orchard and pick fruit that's in season—like apples and pumpkins in fall, or berries in summer. Check out pickyourown.org for options near you.

At some farms in the fall besides picking pumpkins, there are giant corn mazes and rides on hay wagons. You'll find the "World's Largest Corn Maze" at **Richardson Adventure Farm** (richardson adventurefarm.com) in Illinois.

DID YOU KNOW?

Fall is the best time to camp at some campgrounds. From apple picking to Oktoberfest to Halloween, campgrounds often have weekends full of fun autumn festivities.

Festivals and state fairs go on rain or shine usually, except during the pandemic or natural disaster. See what's happening near where you're camping. Have you ever tried fried butter on stick? You can if you are at the Iowa State Fair (iowastatefair.org).

The best way to guarantee a good time, even if the weather is bad, is to make sure you have the right clothing. Bring plenty of layers with you on your trip. It's good to have an umbrella and waterproof boots if there is rain in the forecast. Bring a fleece, a good rain jacket, a light down jacket or vest, a warm hat and light gloves, wool socks, and long underwear. Staying warm and dry is the key to having the most adventures!

Ready for a challenge? Do something you never thought you'd do on a camping trip.

Having fun yet?

{ What's Cool? Seeing the harvest moon while camping. Harvest moon is the name given to the full moon that takes place closest to the autumnal equinox, which falls in late September or early October. The moon turns bright orange and looks like a giant pumpkin.

Staying Safe

How did your parents get lost?

Whether you are on a trail, exploring a city, shopping in a tourist town for souvenirs, or visiting a zoo or a museum, it's easy to get separated from your parents. Here's what you need to do to be prepared if this happens:

- Practice what-if situations with your parents. What should you do if you get separated in a museum? A store? Outdoors in a town or city? Who should you ask for help?

- If you have a phone, you'll have your parents' cell numbers on hand. If not, write their names and phone numbers on a card and put it in your pocket—along with the information for the campground where you are staying. This is especially important for younger siblings who may think your mom and dad's names are "Mommy" and "Daddy."

- Decide in advance on a time and easy-to-locate spot to meet in case you get separated.

- Never approach a vehicle unless you know the driver and are accompanied by an adult.

- Only ask uniformed people for help—police officers, firefighters, store security guards, museum officials, or park rangers.

A COLORADO KID SAYS:
"It's pretty in fall with all the leaves changing colors."
—Maggie, 12

Souvenir Smarts

What's in your collection?

Pencils, patches, stickers, pins . . . a collection of things from the places you've visited make great souvenirs. Sew the patches or put the pins on your backpack. How many do you have from national parks?

Before you go souvenir hunting:

- Talk to your parents about how much you can spend. Do you have birthday money? Some families save loose change in a big jar all year and then divide it up for souvenir shopping.

- Consider if you want one big souvenir or several smaller things along the way.

- Choose something that is made locally, if you can.

- Think about what you have seen or done on the trip and get something that will remind you of that experience—socks with moose on them from Maine, a T-shirt from the California surf shop where you had a lesson, a book from the national park you visited, a mini Liberty Bell from Philadelphia or a Statue of Liberty in New York, a poster from the museum you really liked.

- A picture frame from the region you are visiting is a great family souvenir—make sure you take a family photo!

A KOA NEW YORK CAMPING KID SAYS:
"I think the best part of camping is making memories with families and friends. People should try camping because they're going to want to keep going, because it's so fun."
—Julia, 10, Canandaigua/ Rochester KOA Holiday

Factory Fun

How are jellybeans made? Potato chips? Crayons? You can find out by visiting a factory—an especially good bet on a rainy day! Check out Factory Tour USA (factorytoursusa.com) to find one near where you are camping. Here are six you will especially like:

- **Cape Cod Potato Chip Factory** (capecodchips.com/about/factory-tour)

- **Celestial Seasons Tea Tour** (celestialseasonings.com)

- **Crayola Experience** (crayolaexperience.com/easton)

- **Ben & Jerry's Factory Tour** (benjerry.com/waterbury)

- **Jelly Belly Factory Tour** (jellybelly.com/california-factory-tours)

DID YOU KNOW?

Colorado has North America's largest elk herd—260,000! In the summer they graze in the high mountains. When it gets cold, they move to lower elevations and at dusk you might see them grazing in the meadows. In the fall their loud calls are called "bugles" and mean it's time for the mating season. Estes Park has an annual Elk Fest (estes-park.com/event/elk-fest) every October. There's even a contest to see who sounds most like an elk!

TELL THE ADULTS: MUSEUM FUN

No matter where you are, the weather won't always cooperate. It might be too cold for the beach, raining, or, in the fall in the mountains, even snowing.

The good news is that will give you a chance to do something you might not otherwise have done—like checking out a museum. Consider:

- a museum focused on the region, like **The Journey Museum and Learning Center** (journeymuseum .org) in Rapid City, South Dakota;

- a history museum, like **The Museum of the American Revolution** (amrevmuseum.org) in Philadelphia, Pennsylvania;

- an art museum, like **The Denver Art Museum** (denverart museum.org), where kids up to 18 are admitted free; or

- an interactive science center, like the **Exploratorium** (exploratorium.edu) in San Francisco.

Encourage the kids to do a virtual tour in advance. Each member of the family should pick one exhibit they most want to see so that everyone in the family is happy. Many museums and science centers also offer great virtual family activities.

See if there are special programs or tours for kids and families available. Often there are special tours, interactive projects, and special discovery areas.

If you are going to an art museum, ask the kids where they would be and what they would be doing if they could step inside a painting.

Using the key, write the letters under the symbols to figure out the secret quote. Clue: John Muir, a conservationist and "Father of the National Parks," said this!

For example: 🚲 🌉 🚉 ✈ = b i r d

___ ___ _____

___ _____

___ __ _____ __

a= ✔   b= 🚲   c= 🏙   d= ✈   e= 🎁

f= 🏭   g= 🏛   h= 🏠   i= 🌉   j= 🏚

k= 🌿   l= ?   m= 🗿   n= 👁   o= ⛴

p= 🌲   q= ⛰   r= 🚉   s= ✦   t= ✉

u= 📢   v= 🧭   w= ⛳   x= 🔊   y= ♥

z= 🐝   .= ◼   != 🚌   ,= 🛠

See page 122 for the answer!

Now try and make your own secret messages in the space below.

A MAINE KID SAYS:
"I like the fall here. The bugs are pretty much gone . . . you can go biking and hiking and kayaking and there aren't loads of people. It's pretty peaceful!"
—Annaka, 14

What a
Camping Trip!

I went camping from

_____, _____, 20____ until _____, _____, 20____.

I went camping with . . .

_____

_____

_____

_____

We traveled _____ miles, _____ hours to get to the campsite.

_____

_____

_____

I camped at . . .

_____

_____

_____

I slept in . . .

_____

_____

_____

The weather was . . .

_____

_____

_____

We ate . . .

_____

_____

_____

My favorite thing about camping was . . .

_____

_____

_____

We had the most fun . . .

_____

_____

_____

Next time we go camping, I want to . . .

_____

_____

_____

When I get home, I will miss . . .

_____

_____

_____

I'm excited to get home to . . .

_____

_____

_____

The coolest thing I saw was . . .

_____

_____

_____

The animals that I saw were . . .

_____

_____

_____

Camping was so much fun! Here are some pictures I drew or photos I took of my trip!

REMEMBER ALL YOUR CAMPING TRIPS!

When?	Where?	Who?	I slept in . . .	The best part was . . .

Answer Keys

CHAPTER 1

Welcome to the Campsite! (p. 12)

Fill in the missing letters to spell out the mystery words. (You will need to use some of the secret letters twice!)

(T)OY HAULER
(3)

GUY L(I)NES
     (2)

FULL (H)OOKUP
     (5)

(P)OTABLE
(1)

B(E)AR BAG
  (8)

(C)ARABINER
(4)

KO(A) C(A)MPGROUND
   (6)   (6)

S(N)OWBIRD
  (7)

P	I	T	C	H	A	T	E	N	T
(1)	(2)	(3)	(4)	(5)	(6)	(3)	(8)	(7)	(3)

Connect the Dots! (p. 13)
CAMPFIRE

CHAPTER 2

What Do You See on the Road? Word Search (p. 25)

H	R	E	S	T	M	V	S	A	Q
L	E	V	K	O	M	H	I	U	R
I	T	M	R	C	H	T	N	D	E
C	S	L	U	L	W	T	G	L	S
E	G	V	A	M	H	F	A	J	T
N	C	O	G	P	Y	S	L	K	S
S	V	E	W	I	G	M	O	A	T
E	K	O	M	J	U	H	N	U	O
G	P	I	C	N	I	C	G	D	P
J	M	K	Z	R	M	A	S	I	X
N	A	N	O	F	N	R	A	O	S
S	N	A	C	K	S	A	O	B	G
U	G	P	S	W	Z	V	K	O	S
C	P	S	W	U	M	A	F	O	J
S	G	S	S	E	W	N	D	K	B
N	A	V	I	G	A	T	O	R	C
E	R	S	X	T	V	F	H	Z	S
A	I	R	S	T	R	E	A	M	S
H	R	E	S	T	M	V	S	A	H
E	G	V	A	M	H	F	A	J	O
S	V	E	W	I	G	M	O	A	P
Q	W	F	C	F	Z	Y	F	A	X
S	G	S	J	B	C	S	S	H	O

CHAPTER 3

Campsite Crossword (p. 37)

Across

1) Corn chips or anything else dry and crinkly can work in a pinch. KINDLING
2) The best campsite neighbors are . . . QUIET
3) A home on wheels that you brought from home. CAMPER

Down

4) Keeps things cool and fights dehydration. ICE
5) A must-have for dog walking. LEASH
6) If you don't have a flashlight, grab a . . . LANTERN
7) The first thing you need to make a campfire. FIREWOOD

CHAPTER 5

Match the National Park to the State (p. 57)

Acadia National Park . . . . Maine

Yosemite National Park. . . . . California

Glacier National Park . . . . Montana

Yellowstone National Park . . . . Wyoming

Big Bend National Park. . . . . Texas

Shenandoah National Park . . . . Virginia

Grand Canyon National Park. . . . . Arizona

Rocky Mountain National Park. . . . . Colorado

Olympic National Park . . . . Washington

Cuyahoga Valley National Park . . . . Ohio

It's a Word Safari! Word Search (p. 79)

```
Q  O  Y  V  J  X  Q  Q  A  E
W  N  Y  W  T  E  Y  V  M  W
F  L  A  S  H  L  I  G  H  T
C  K  G  V  W  Q  I  K  D  T
F  U  J  G  B  P  X  V  L  I
Z  R  R  N  Z  K  S  Z  C  S
Y  A  G  Z  G  H  V  E  T  S
F  B  U  G  S  P  R  A  Y  U
A  H  K  W  C  Q  T  I  F  E
X  J  Z  U  Y  K  N  N  R  S
S  L  K  Z  L  E  Y  Y  N  W
G  B  O  T  F  P  P  I  G  J
S  U  N  G  L  A  S  S  E  S
J  R  X  K  W  T  B  K  Y  X
B  J  H  Z  T  E  C  P  T  N
C  A  M  E  R  A  D  O  M  W
S  C  L  F  I  B  V  E  S  A
S  K  L  C  P  S  K  G  E  T
H  E  M  H  B  W  Y  B  Q  E
O  T  J  C  A  N  S  G  V  R
P  B  W  G  G  N  M  A  P  C
O  R  V  X  W  U  J  Q  O  W
Z  H  L  J  V  F  O  J  L  C
```

CHAPTER 8

Secret Decoder (p. 91)

WINDSURFING

CANOEING

KAYAK

PADDLEBOARD

CHAPTER 10

Secret Quote Puzzle (p. 111)

The mountains are calling and I must go.

About the Author

Award-winning author **Eileen Ogintz** is a leading national family travel expert whose syndicated "Taking the Kids" is the most widely distributed column in the country on family travel. She has also created TakingtheKids.com, which helps families make the most of their vacations together. Ogintz is the author of seven family travel books and is often quoted in major publications such as *USA Today,* the *Wall Street Journal,* and the *New York Times,* as well as parenting and women's magazines on family travel. She has appeared on such television programs as *The Today Show, Good Morning America,* and *The Oprah Winfrey Show,* as well as dozens of local radio and television news programs. She has traveled around the world with her three children and others in the family, talking to traveling families wherever she goes. She is also the author of *The Kid's Guide to New York City; The Kid's Guide to Orlando; The Kid's Guide to Washington, DC; The Kid's Guide to Chicago; The Kid's Guide to Denver, Boulder & Colorado Ski Country; The Kid's Guide to Los Angeles County; The Kid's Guide to San Diego; The Kid's Guide to San Francisco; The Kid's Guide to the Great Smoky Mountains;* and *The Kid's Guide to Boston* (all Globe Pequot Press); as well as *The Kid's Guide to Maine* and *The Kid's Guide to Acadia National Park* (Down East Books).

About KOA

Kampgrounds of America (KOA) is the world's largest family camping company. Founded in 1962, they have more than 500 campground locations in North America. From humble beginnings on the banks of the Yellowstone River in Billings, Montana, KOA has become an iconic brand throughout the US and Canada. Their "Yellow Sign" acts as a beacon of fun and relaxation for campers, and a badge of honor for KOA employees. Guests have come to know KOA for their superior service and amazing amenities. Learn more or find a KOA location at KOA.com.